Simply Suspense

FRANK STOCKTON, STACY AUMONIER and ALFRED BURRAGE

Level 2

Retold by J.Y. K. Kerr
Series Editors: Andy Hopkins and Jocelyn Potter

Pearson Education Limited
Edinburgh Gate, Harlow,
Essex CM20 2JE, England
and Associated Companies throughout the world.

ISBN: 978-1-4058-6948-5

The Lady or The Tiger? was first published in 1884, 'Miss Bracegirdle's
Night of Fear' was first published as *Miss Bracegirdle Does Her Duty and
Other Stories* in 1923 and 'The Waxwork' was first published as *Someone
in the Room* in 1931
This adaptation first published by Penguin Books 1991
Published by Addison Wesley Longman Ltd and Penguin Books Ltd 1998
This edition first published 2008

1 3 5 7 9 10 8 6 4 2

Text copyright © J.Y.K. Kerr 1991
Illustrations copyright © Richard Johnson 1991
This edition copyright © Pearson Education Ltd 2008
Illustrations by Tudor Humphries

The moral right of the adapter and of the illustrator has been asserted

Typeset by Graphicraft Ltd, Hong Kong
Set in 11/14pt Bembo
Printed in China
SWTC/01

Published by Pearson Education Ltd in association with
Penguin Books Ltd, both companies being subsidiaries of Pearson Plc

Contents

Introduction

But no scream came out of her mouth. Her fear was much too strong. She stayed very quiet and listened. Was he going to hit her...?

Are you sometimes afraid? These three stories are about fear.

'The Lady or the Tiger?' happens in a strange country. The King's daughter and the King's gardener are in love. The King does not know. But one day he finds them in the garden and he is very angry. What will happen to the gardener? Will he live or will he die?

An Englishwoman is staying in a hotel in south-west France in 'Miss Bracegirdle's Night of Fear'. She goes into her room and finds...a strange man asleep in the bed. She tries to leave the room, but she can't get out! She is very afraid. Will he wake up? What will she do?

'The Waxwork' happens in a small English town. The year is 1931. A newspaper man is going to write a story about a night in a waxworks. He sits in a chair in a room of murderers. The night begins. It is quiet and dark...but then things start to move.

Frank Stockton (1834–1902) was born in Philadelphia, USA. He enjoyed telling stories. He wrote a lot of books and short stories. 'The Lady or the Tiger?' was his most famous work. People in America talked about it for years. American schoolchildren study it today.

Stacy Aumonier (1887–1928) was an English writer. His most famous story was 'The Friends', about two drinkers. He was ill for a long time, and he was only forty-one when he died.

Alfred Burrage (1889–1956) wrote his first short story when he was sixteen. Then he wrote hundreds more. Readers in America liked 'The Waxwork' very much. Twenty years later he made it into a story for television.

The Lady or the Tiger?

Many, many years ago there was a king in a far country. He was famous, he was strong and he was very clever. But in his country he had many wrongdoers. The King was unhappy about this but how can you stop people from doing wrong? It is not easy. He thought about this difficult question for a long time but he could not find the answer.

Suddenly, one day, he had a good idea. He spoke to his people and told them to build a big stadium in the centre of the city.

'It must be very big and very beautiful,' he told them.

So the people worked hard for many months.

One day, the building was finished. The stadium was ready. Inside it, there were places for five thousand people. Everyone was very excited about this beautiful new building. Some wanted to watch games in the stadium. Others wanted to have dancing and singing. But what did the King want? No one knew.

The day of the opening came. Everyone ran to the stadium to get a place inside. The people got more excited when the King arrived. They were all quiet, waiting. First, he took his place. Then, he stood up and spoke.

'My people, my friends,' he said. 'Firstly I want to thank all the workers for their good work. We now have a beautiful stadium and it is very well built. Secondly, I know that many of you want to see games and dancing here. But this stadium is going to be different. It is not going to be a place for having a good time. It is going to be a place for wrongdoers. If one of you does something wrong, we are going to bring him to this place. There he must stand in the middle of this stadium in front of us all.

'Now, do you all see those two doors, coloured blue, at the

far end of the stadium? They look the same, perhaps. But they are not. Behind one door, I am going to put a dangerous animal, a tiger. Behind the other door, there is going to be a beautiful lady. The wrongdoer must choose one of these doors. If he opens the wrong door, he finds the tiger. It jumps out and kills him. If he opens the other door, he finds the beautiful young woman. She is to be his wife. They must marry immediately, right here in the stadium before our eyes. After that, they can live happily with us as husband and wife. So each wrongdoer must choose very carefully. Before he chooses, he – and we – cannot know if he is going to live or die. As soon as he opens one of those two doors, we all know immediately. That is my idea. So tell me, my friends, is it a good idea or is it not?'

'It is good, O King, it is very good,' the people answered. But they were quiet. They were afraid.

'Thank you,' said the King. 'Now go home. Come to the stadium again at the same time next week. Then you can watch the first wrongdoer make his choice. Every week from now on, a different man is going to choose: to live, if he is lucky, or to die, if he is not.'

From that day, the people came every week to the stadium to watch a different wrongdoer. Sometimes, he opened the right blue door and the beautiful lady came out. Then there was singing and dancing. Everyone threw flowers down to the lucky people and went home happily. But at other times, the wrongdoer opened the wrong door. Immediately, a big tiger ran out into the stadium and jumped on the unlucky man. In a few minutes, the tiger killed him in front of all the watching people. When he lay dead in the centre of the stadium, the people went home sadly. They took their flowers with them. It is interesting that in a short time the number of wrongdoers in the country got much smaller. No one wanted

If the wrongdoer opens the wrong door, he finds the tiger. It jumps out and kills him.

to stand in the middle of the stadium and make that difficult choice.

Now, there is another important person in this story. The King had only one child, a daughter. She was very beautiful. She had green eyes and long red hair and she moved as quickly as a cat. She too was strong and clever – as strong and clever as her father. She did not smile often. But when she smiled, people were happy. When she was angry, everyone was afraid. They knew that at those times she was a very dangerous young woman. Her picture was in every home. Men, women and children followed her when she went walking in the streets of the city. They waited to see her famous smile and sometimes they were lucky.

One day, she was out walking in a city park when she saw a young man. He was a gardener and the park was where he worked. He was very good-looking. He was tall and strong. He had dark blue-black hair and a dark moustache. When he laughed, you could see his beautiful white teeth. The King's daughter stopped and looked at him closely. She thought that he was the most beautiful man in the world. She began to talk with him and liked him more and more. The young man could not understand. Why did the King's daughter want to talk to him? He was not important. He was only the King's gardener. But he could not take his eyes off her. As soon as he looked into her big green eyes and saw her smile, he was in love. But he knew that this love was very dangerous. He was not a rich man, not from a rich family. He could never marry the daughter of the King.

But the two young lovers knew that they must meet again. They started to meet every day, at times when no one could see them. Every day, their love was stronger and stronger. They were very happy. Then one day the King found them together, there in the city gardens. His daughter was in the young

The king's daughter thought that the gardener was the most beautiful man in the world.

Then one day the King found them together, there in the city gardens. His daughter was in the young man's arms.

man's arms. The King was very, very angry. He called his men. Immediately, they took the young man away and shut him in a dark, dirty room. They gave him only bread and water to eat. Now the King's daughter could not see her lover any more. The young man lay in the dark. He knew that he was a wrongdoer and in much danger from the King.

Now, we know that the King's daughter was a strong young woman and that she was very clever. When her father's men took her lover away, she too saw the danger immediately. She knew very well what was going to happen next. So, early in the morning, she went to the stadium. No one saw her go. She spoke to the workers there and gave them some money.

'Which room is the tiger in?' she asked.

They told her.

'And which girl is going to be behind the other door?'

The workers did not want to answer. They were afraid.

'I must know,' said the King's daughter. 'Who is she?'

'She is the daughter of your father's driver,' the workers answered.

The King's daughter knew her well: a young and beautiful girl with rich brown hair. But the King's daughter did not like her. She began to think hard. 'If my lover chooses the wrong door, he dies. But if he chooses the right door, he marries this cheap little thing, this driver's child. And I lose him – to her! So I too must choose . . .'

That afternoon, the King called all his people back to the stadium again. His men brought the young man from the dark room. There he stood, in the middle of the stadium, tired, hungry and afraid. The King sat in his place above the people and his daughter sat next to him. She did not move. Her face showed nothing.

Then the King stood and spoke to his people. 'You all know this gardener, my friends. And you know why he is here. He was the lover of my daughter. For many weeks, I did not know that; but I know it now. What happens to a wrongdoer in our country? That too we know. He must choose: the lady or the tiger. If he opens the wrong door, he must fight the tiger. If he opens the right door, he must marry the lady. So now choose, young man. Choose very carefully if you want to live and not die.'

The young man stood quietly and listened to the King's words. But his eyes were not on the King. They were on the face of the King's daughter. She had no smile for him today.

Her eyes told him something. She looked quickly at her hand.
Her finger moved a little to the left.

But he looked at her eyes. Her eyes told him something. She looked down quickly at her hand. Then she looked up again. He saw her smallest finger move a little to the left. And immediately he knew: the door to open was the door on the left! He turned and walked very slowly to the left-hand door. All the people watched him, without a sound. He put out his hand and opened the door...

But here the story ends. Remember that the King's daughter was a clever young woman. She was in love but she was angry too. Did she want her lover to meet the tiger – a fight that he must lose? Did she want him to die? Or did she want him to live and have another beautiful woman for his wife? To give him this other woman, in place of her? We do not know what ideas were at work inside her beautiful head.

Tell me, what do you think? Which did she choose? What was behind that door: the lady or the tiger?

Miss Bracegirdle's Night of Fear

'This is the room, madame.'

'Oh thank you – thank you.'

'Does madame like the room?'

'Oh yes. Thank you. It is very nice.'

'Does madame want anything more?'

'If it is not too late, I want to have a hot bath.'

'That is quite easy, madame. The bathroom is the room at the end of this floor, on the left. I can get the bath ready for madame.'

'There is just one more thing. I came by train from England today, so I am very tired. Please do not bring my breakfast too early tomorrow. I want to have a good sleep tonight.'

'I understand, madame.'

The girl went off to get the bath ready.

Millicent Bracegirdle was right. She was tired. She thought of Easingstoke, her home town, now so far away. She remembered the drive to London early that morning; the train from London to Dover; the boat to Calais. Then another train to Paris. By lunchtime, she was in a third train, going from Paris to Bordeaux. Now, here she was in the hotel. It was twelve o'clock at night. Why was she here in south-west France, of all places? It was all because of Annie, her younger sister. Annie usually lived in South America. Earlier in the year, Annie got ill and now she was to have a holiday in Europe. Miss Bracegirdle's brother could not come to meet Annie off the boat: he had too much work to do in Easingstoke. So Miss Bracegirdle was the only other person.

'The ship is going to arrive in Bordeaux tomorrow,' thought Miss Bracegirdle. 'And I am going to see Annie again after all these years.'

The girl showed her the room. 'Does madame like the room?'
she asked.

This was Miss Bracegirdle's first visit to France. She did not usually take holidays away from home. Luckily she spoke a little French. 'It is not so difficult to live in France,' she thought. 'The thing to understand is that it is quite different from Easingstoke.'

She took her things one by one out of her bag and put them away carefully. She thought about her home in Easingstoke, with flowers in all the rooms and photographs of the family. She thought about her poor brother, working so hard. She felt a little sad, but only for a minute. Her time in France was to be quite short. She was going to be home again soon. Now she must get a good night's sleep. But first that hot bath . . .

She took off her day things and put on her nightdress. Then she picked up her washing things and went to the bathroom, closing her bedroom door quietly. She lay in the hot water and thought about the nice young girl in the hotel, getting her bath ready. People in this hotel were very friendly – always ready to help. There was so much she wanted to tell her brother when she got home.

She got out of the bath and put on her nightdress again. She cleaned the bath very carefully. She did not want French people to think that the English were dirty. Then she left the bathroom and went back to her bedroom. She went in quickly, put on the light and shut the door.

Then, one of those unlucky things happened: the handle of the door came off in her hand. She tried to put the handle back on the door but she could not. 'How do I do it?' she thought. 'It is going to be very difficult to open the door now. Do I ask that nice girl to come and help me? Perhaps by now she is in bed.'

She turned away from the door, and suddenly, she saw something much, much worse than the door-handle. There was

There was a man in her bed! She felt quite ill with fear.

a man in her bed! She took one look at his thick black hair and his big black moustache and immediately felt quite ill with fear. For a minute or two, she could not think. Then her first thought was: 'I must not scream!' She stood there but she could not move. She just looked at the man's dark head and the big line of his back under the bedthings. She began to think very quickly. Her next thought was: 'I am in the wrong room. It is the man's room.' She could see his jacket and trousers lying on a chair and his big black shoes on the floor. She must get out quickly. But how? She tried again to open the door with her fingers but she could not.

Here she was, shut in a hotel room with an unknown man – a Frenchman! She must think, she must think! She turned off the light. 'Perhaps with the light off, he is not going to wake up,' she thought. 'That gives me more time to do something. But if he does wake up, what do I do? He is not going to believe my story. Nobody is going to believe me. In England perhaps but not here. How can they understand? So, I must get out of this room. By waking him? By screaming? By calling the young girl? No, it is no good. If I scream or call out, people are going to come running immediately. And what do they find? Miss Bracegirdle from Easingstoke in a man's bedroom after twelve o'clock at night. Just think of all the talk back home when my friends hear about that! And if I climb out of the window?' She thought of the big hairy man pulling her back by the legs as she tried to get out. He could wake up at any minute. She thought that she heard somebody going past outside the door. But it was too late to scream now.

Suddenly, she had an idea. It was now nearly one o'clock in the morning. Perhaps the sleeping man was not dangerous. At seven or eight o'clock, he must get up and go out to work. 'I can get under the bed and wait there until he goes. Men never look under the bed. When he sees the door-handle on the floor, he is going to open the door with something or call the girl to come. Later, I can come out from under the bed and go quietly back to my room. Nobody is going to know.'

She lay down on the floor and got under the bed. No sound came from the man above her, but from down here it was difficult to hear anything. She tried to think of her nice little bedroom in Easingstoke with its nice white bed but the floor was getting harder every minute. She tried to think what her room number was. One hundred and fifteen? Or was it one

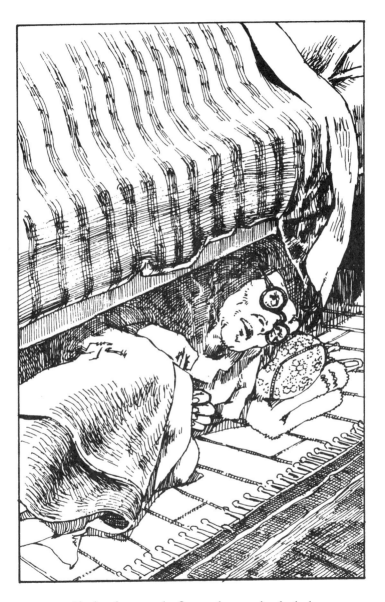

She lay down on the floor and got under the bed.

hundred and sixteen? She was always bad at remembering numbers. She began to think of her schooldays and the interesting things she learned then. Suddenly, she felt that she was going to sneeze. She could not stop it. The sneeze came – a long, hard one. 'This is the end of me,' Miss Bracegirdle thought. 'Now this Frenchman is going to jump out of bed and turn on the light. Then he is going to look under the bed and pull me out. And then . . . And then? What can I do then? I can scream if he puts his hands on me. Perhaps it is better to scream first, before that happens. If not, he can put his hand over my mouth and stop me from screaming.'

But no scream came out of her mouth. Her fear was much too strong. She stayed very quiet and listened. Was he going to hit her – with one of those heavy shoes, perhaps? But nothing happened. Miss Bracegirdle suddenly knew that she could not stay under that bed a minute longer. It was better to come out, wake up the man and tell him everything. With difficulty she got out from under the bed and stood up. She went over to the door and put on the light. She turned to the bed and said, as strongly as she could, 'Monsieur!'

Nothing happened. She looked at the man and said again, 'Monsieur! Monsieur!'

But again there was no answer. She went closer to the bed. His hair and moustache were very black but his face had no colour in it. His mouth was open but his eyes were shut.

Then for the third time that night, Miss Bracegirdle nearly died of fear. Suddenly, her legs felt as weak as water. She nearly fell down. Because the man in the bed was dead! It was the first time that she stood face to face with a dead person, but there was no mistake. The man was dead. Miss Bracegirdle could only say, 'He's dead! He's dead!'

Her difficulties now were not important. She began to feel

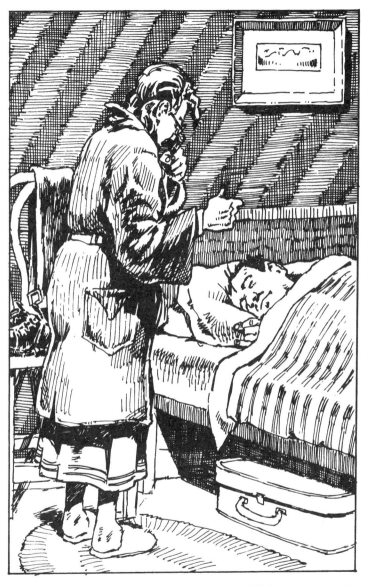

*Miss Bracegirdle nearly died of fear. She nearly fell down. Because the
man in the bed was dead!*

sorry for him, lying here dead in a hotel room. But a sudden sound broke into her thoughts. Somebody outside the door put down some shoes: the shoe-cleaning boy. She heard the sound of his feet die away and remembered where she was. To be in an unknown man's bedroom was bad, but to be in a room with a dead man was much, much worse! If they found her here, people were going to think she killed him! A picture came into her head: the police taking her off to the police station, asking her questions, shutting her away... And her sister arriving in just a few hours' time too! She must get out of the room immediately. 'I cannot call for help now,' she thought, fighting back her fear. 'Do something, Millicent. It is now or never!'

But what? She went round the room, looking for something to open the door with. She could find nothing. Finally, she picked up the man's jacket. Inside it she found a small knife. She took the knife and put it in the side of the door. Very slowly she turned the knife and the door opened.

She wanted to run out of the room immediately but she stopped first and listened. Nobody was there. Feeling very afraid, Miss Bracegirdle shut the door quickly behind her and ran as fast as she could to her bedroom. She lay down on the bed and the fear slowly began to leave her. All was well! But then she had another unhappy thought. The living fear came back. Her washing things were in there. They were lying there in the dead man's room! And her name was on them. To go back again now was far worse than the first time but she had no choice. She could not leave her things lying there. 'If they find them, they are going to ask me how they got there,' she thought. She had to go back.

She went. She did not look at the bed. She quickly took her washing things and ran back again to her bedroom. Now that the danger was over, she suddenly felt very, very tired. She got

She took the knife and put it in the side of the door. Very slowly, she turned the knife and the door opened.

into bed and put out the light. She lay in the dark, trying to forget her fears. Finally, she went to sleep.

It was eleven o'clock when she woke up. The sun was high in the sky and the fears of the night were far away. In the light of the day, it was all very difficult to believe. Miss Bracegirdle tried to think about other things.

Finally, the young girl arrived to wake her up. Her eyes showed that she was excited. 'Oh, madame!' she said, 'a very bad thing happened here last night. The man in room one hundred and seventeen – he is dead! Please do not say that I told you but the police were here, the doctor, everybody.'

Miss Bracegirdle said nothing. There was nothing to say. But the young woman was too excited to stop. 'And do you know who this dead man was, madame? They say that he was Boldhu, the famous killer, wanted by the police. Last year, he killed a woman and cut her up and threw her into the river. And last night, he died here in our hotel – in the room next door! We do not know how. Did you say coffee, madame?'

'No thank you, just a cup of tea – strong tea, please.'

'Very well, madame.'

The girl left and soon a man from the kitchen came with Miss Bracegirdle's cup of tea. Miss Bracegirdle thought that this was unusual: a man bringing tea to a lady's bedroom. These things did not happen in Easingstoke. But French people were different. She thought about the man in the next room. She felt quite sorry for him now, dying so suddenly, far from home.

She got up, washed and dressed. After that, she took her pen and some paper and went down to the hotel sitting-room. Nobody in the hotel was very excited. Perhaps they did not know about the dead man. She went to the writing-table and started to write her letter:

Hotel Carlton
Bordeaux

5 September

My dear brother,

I hope you are well. I arrived here late last night. The time in the train was long but quite interesting. I nearly lost my glasses but a nice man found them for me. The people here are very friendly but the food is quite different from English food. I am going to meet Annie at one o'clock. I remembered in the train that

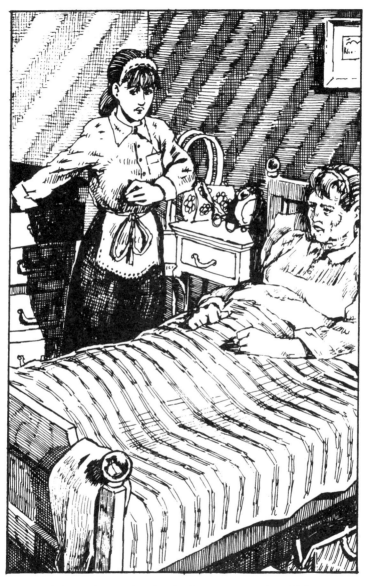

'And do you know who this dead man was, madame? They say that he is Boldhu, the famous killer.'

there is some fruit from Mrs Hunt's garden in the kitchen cupboard. I forgot to tell Lizzie about it, so please tell her for me. I do not want it to go bad. This is a nice hotel but I think that Annie and I are going to move to the Grand Hotel tonight, because the rooms here are not very quiet. That is all there is to tell you for now. Be careful not to get cold. I am coming back soon.

Your loving sister,
Millicent.

She could not tell her brother about last night, not in the letter and not when she got home. It was too difficult to say how she came to be in a man's bedroom – an unknown man, a dead man. Or about getting under his bed. Or about opening the door with his knife. Her brother always felt unhappy if anything unusual happened to her. It was much better not to say anything. She put on her hat and coat and went out to send the letter. The sun was warm. It was good to walk in the streets. There were a lot of people in the cafes, laughing, talking, moving about. They were so different from the people in Easingstoke. It was exciting to be in France.

'I was in a Frenchman's bedroom all last night,' she suddenly thought. She smiled.

Miss Bracegirdle walked more quickly to the letter-box to send her letter. Her face was a little red but perhaps only because it was a warm day. She put her letter in the box and waited to hear it fall inside. It fell. So that was that. She turned and went to meet her sister off the boat from South America.

Miss Bracegirdle walked to the letter-box to send her letter. Her face
was a little red but perhaps only because it was a warm day.

The Waxwork

It was closing time at Marriner's Waxworks. The last few visitors came out in twos and threes through the big glass doors. But Mr Marriner, the boss, sat in his office, talking to a caller, Raymond Hewson. Hewson was a thin man, carefully but poorly dressed. He spoke well but seemed to be losing his fight to do well in the world.

Marriner began to speak, in answer to a question from his visitor.

'Please don't think that what you're asking for is anything new,' he said. 'A lot of people ask to stay the night in our Murderers' Room. We always say no, because it does nothing for us. But you are a writer. Now that's quite different. We like people to read about us. It helps to bring in more visitors – and more money.

'That's just what I thought,' said Hewson. 'I knew that you wanted my help.'

Marriner laughed. 'Oh I know what you're going to say next. Somebody told me that Madame Tussaud's★ gives people one hundred pounds to stay the night in their Murderers' Room. But you mustn't think that we're as rich as they are. Tell me, what newspaper do you work for, Mr Hewson?'

'Oh I work for any newspaper that takes what I write,' said Hewson carefully: 'I know that I can easily sell this story. *The Morning Times* takes anything to do with murderers. Just think: "A Night with Marriner's Murderers". Every newspaper is going to want that!'

★ Madame Tussaud's is a place in England that is famous for its wax figures.

It was closing time at Marriner's Waxworks. Mr Marriner, the boss, sat in his office talking to a caller, Raymond Hewson.

Marriner thought for a minute. 'Very well, Mr Hewson, let's say this. If your story comes out in *The Morning Times*, there's five pounds waiting for you here the next day. But please understand it's not easy, what you want to do. I know all about our wax-works, you see. I walk past them hundreds of times every day. But spend a night down there with all those figures? No thank you!'

'Why not?' asked Hewson.

'It's difficult to say. I don't like the idea, that's all. You're not going to have an easy night, you know.'

Hewson knew that only too well. But he smiled, not wanting to show his feelings. He remembered his wife and family. He must work hard because of them. They had not got much money left, this month. He must not lose this lucky opening. That newspaper was going to pay him well for this story. And then there was the five pounds from Marriner too. Perhaps if he wrote a good story, the newspaper had more work to give him. But he must do this story well first.

'Murderers often have a hard time but we writers have our difficulties too,' he said, laughing. 'Your Murderers' Room is no hotel bedroom. But I don't think your waxworks are going to make me too unhappy.'

'You don't feel afraid then?'

'Oh no,' laughed Hewson.

Mr Marriner smiled and stood up. 'Right,' he said. 'The last people are all out now. Wait a minute. I want to tell the man down there not to put the covers on the waxworks. And to tell our night people that you're going to be down below. Then I can show you round.'

He picked up a telephone and spoke into it. Then he said, 'There's just one thing I must ask. There was some talk of a fire down in the Murderers' Room earlier this evening. I don't know who said there was a fire but it seems it was a mistake. So please don't smoke. Now if you're ready, let's make a move.

Hewson followed Marriner through five or six rooms where his men were at work covering up the kings of England and other famous people. Marriner spoke to one of the men, asking him to bring an armchair to the Murderers' Room.

'I'm sorry but that's the best we can do,' he said. 'Perhaps if you sit in the chair, you can get some sleep.'

He took the writer down to the Murderers' Room. It was a big room without much light. Hewson thought of a church: you felt you had to speak very quietly in here. But this was not a good place. It was a place for remembering wrongdoers, murderers and the bad things that made them famous.

The waxwork figures stood on small stands, with numbers at

Mr Marriner took Raymond Hewson to the Murderers' Room.

their feet. He knew some of the figures but not others. There stood Thurtell, the murderer of Weir. Over there was little Lefroy, a killer hungry for money. Five yards away sat Mrs Thompson, known for her unusual lovers. Browne and Kennedy, the two newest figures, stood next to Mrs Dyer and Patrick Mahon.

Marriner showed Hewson the more interesting murderers one by one. 'That's Crippen, as you perhaps know. A weak little man, not very interesting to look at. There's old Vaquier. You can tell him by all that hair on his face. And this is –'

'Yes, who's that?' asked Hewson quietly.

'Oh he's the best figure in our show. Of all these people, he's the only one living today.'

Hewson looked at the waxwork closely: a small, thin figure only five feet tall. It had a little moustache, big glasses and an unusual coat. It was easy to see that he was French. Without knowing why, he felt suddenly afraid of that smiling face. He moved back from the figure, finding it difficult to look at it again.

'But who is he?' he asked.

'That,' said Marriner, 'is Dr Bourdette.'

Hewson didn't know the name. Marriner smiled. 'If you're French, you remember it well,' he said. 'For years all Paris was in fear of this little man. He worked as a doctor by day. But at night he cut people's throats. He killed just because he liked killing and always in the same way. After his last murder, the police found some important letters. They know all about him now and if only they can catch him . . .

'But our friend here is too clever for them. He knew the police were after him. They soon lost him. They're looking for him now all over Europe. They think he's dead but they can't find the body. Last year, there were one or two more murders. But the police believe that another person is now doing the

Without knowing why, Raymond Hewson felt suddenly afraid of that smiling face.

killing in his place. It's interesting how every well-known murderer has his followers, isn't it?'

Hewson felt fear run through his body.

'I don't like him much,' he said. 'Just look at those eyes!'

'You find that his eyes eat into you! That's how he did it, you know. He could send people to sleep just with his eyes. In these killings, the murdered person never seemed to fight back. He's too small to kill anybody if they're not sleeping.'

'I thought I saw him move just now,' said Hewson, trying not to show his fear.

Marriner smiled. 'You're going to think that you see many things before the night is over. We're not going to shut you in down here. When you feel it's time to stop, come up again. There are watchmen in the building, so don't be afraid if you hear them moving about. I'm sorry that I can't give you any more light. We like to have the room dark, you understand. Now come back to my office and have a strong drink before starting the night's work.

◆

The night watchman brought the armchair for Hewson. He tried to make him laugh.

'Where do I put it, sir?' he asked. 'Just here? Then you can talk to Dr Crippen, when you get tired of doing nothing. Or there's old Mrs Dyer over there making eyes at you. She usually likes to have a man to talk to. Just tell me where, sir.'

Hewson smiled. The man's words made him feel happier – tonight's work didn't seem quite so difficult.

'I can choose a place for it, thank you,' he said.

'Well, goodnight, sir. I'm on the floor above if you want me. Don't let any of these figures come up behind you and put their cold hands round your throat. And look out for that old Mrs Dyer. I think she finds you interesting.'

The night watchman brought the armchair for Hewson. He tried to make him laugh.

Hewson laughed and said goodnight to the man. After some thought, he put the armchair with its back to Dr Bourdette. He couldn't say why but Bourdette was much worse to look at than the other figures. He felt quite happy as he put the chair in its place. But as the watchman's feet died away, he thought of the long night in front of him. Weak light lit the lines of figures. They seemed near to being living people. The big dark room was very quiet. Hewson wanted to hear the usual sounds of people talking and moving about, but there was nothing. Not a movement. Not a sound.

'I feel I'm on the floor of the sea,' he thought. 'I must remember to put that into my story.'

He looked without much interest at the unmoving figures all round him. But before long, he felt those eyes again, the hard eyes of Bourdette, looking at him from behind. He wanted more and more to turn round and look at the figure.

'This is all wrong,' he thought. 'If I turn round now, it only shows that I'm afraid.'

And then he heard another person speaking inside his head. 'It's just because you *are* afraid, that you can't turn round and look.'

These different thoughts seemed to be fighting inside him.

Finally, Hewson turned his chair a little and looked behind him. Of the many figures standing there, the figure of the little doctor seemed the most important. Perhaps this was because a stronger light came down on the place where he stood. Hewson looked at the face so cleverly made in wax. His eyes met the figure's eyes. He quickly turned away.

'He's only a waxwork, the same as the others,' Hewson said quietly.

They were only waxworks, yes. But waxworks do not move. He didn't see any of them moving. But he did think that now the figures in front of him seemed to be standing a little differently.

The big dark room was very quiet. Hewson wanted to hear the usual sounds of people talking and moving about.

Crippen was one. Was his body turned a little more to the left? 'Or,' he thought, 'perhaps my chair isn't quite in the same place after turning round.'

Hewson stopped looking. He took out a little book and wrote a line or two.

'Everything quiet. Feel I'm on the floor of the sea. Bourdette trying to send me to sleep with his eyes. Figures seem to move when you're not watching.'

He closed the book and quickly looked to his right. He saw only the weak wax face of Lefroy, looking back at him with a sorry smile.

It was just his fears. Or was it? Didn't Crippen move again as he looked away? He just waited for you to take your eyes off him, then made his move. 'That's what they all do. I know it!' he thought. 'It's too much!' He started to get up from his chair. He must leave immediately. He couldn't stay all night with a lot of murderers, moving about when he wasn't looking!

Hewson sat down again. He must not be so jumpy. They were only waxworks, so there was nothing to fear. But why then did he feel so afraid, always thinking that they played games with him? He turned round again quickly and met Bourdette's hard eyes. Then suddenly, he turned back to look at Crippen. Ha! He nearly caught Crippen moving that time. 'Be careful, Crippen – and all you others,' he said. 'If I do catch you moving, I'm going to break your arms and legs off. Do you hear?'

'I can leave now,' he thought. 'I've got a lot to write about. A good story – ten good stories! *The Morning Times* isn't going to know how long I stayed here. They aren't interested. But the watchman is going to laugh if he sees me leaving so early. And then there's the money from Marriner – I don't want to lose that.'

But this was too hard. It was bad that the waxworks moved

behind your back. But it was worse that they could breathe. Or was it just *his* breathing, seeming to come from far away? These figures seemed to be doing what children do in a lesson: talking, laughing and playing when the person giving the lesson turns his back.

'There I go again,' he thought. 'I must think about other things. I'm Raymond Hewson. I live and breathe. These figures round me aren't living. They can't move and speak as I can. They're only made of wax. They just stand there for old ladies and little boys to look at.'

He began to feel better again. He tried to remember a good story a friend told him last week . . .

He remembered some of it but not all. He had the feeling that Bourdette's eyes were on him again. He must have a look. He half-turned and then pulled his chair right round. Now, they were face to face. As he spoke, his words seemed to fly back at him from the darkest corners of the room.

'You moved, you little animal!' he screamed. 'Yes you did. I saw you!'

Then he sat, looking in front of him, not moving, cold with fear. Dr Bourdette moved his little body slowly and carefully. He got down from his stand and sat right in front of Hewson. Then he smiled and said in good English, 'Good evening. I did not know that I was going to have a friend here tonight. Then I heard you and Marriner talking. You cannot move or speak now until I tell you. But you can hear me quite easily, I know. Something tells me that you are – let's say, a little afraid of me. Make no mistake, sir. I am not one of these poor dead figures suddenly turned into a living thing. Oh no. I am Dr Bourdette in person.'

He stopped and moved his legs.

'I am sorry but my arms and legs are quite tired. I don't want to take up your time with my uninteresting story. I can just say that some unusual happenings brought me to England. I was near this building this evening, when I saw a policeman looking at me too closely. I thought perhaps he wanted to ask me some difficult questions, so I quickly came in here with all the other visitors. Then I had a very good idea. I told somebody that I saw smoke. Everybody ran out into the street, thinking there was a fire. I stayed here. I undressed that figure of me, put on its coat and quickly put the figure at the back of the room, where nobody could see it. Then I took its place here on the stand.

'I must say that I had a very tiring evening. But luckily the people didn't watch me all the time. I could breathe sometimes and move my arms and legs a little.

'What Marriner said about me was not very nice, you know. But he was right about one thing – I am not dead. It's important that the world thinks I am. What he said about my doings is mostly right too. Most people, you know, collect something or other. Some collect books, some collect money, others collect pictures or other tickets. And me? I collect throats.'

He stopped talking for a minute and looked at Hewson's throat carefully. He did not seem to think it was a very good one.

'I'm happy you came tonight,' he went on. 'You mustn't think that I don't want you here. It was difficult for me to do any interesting "collecting" over the last few months. So now I'm happy to go back to my usual work. I'm sorry to see that your throat is a little thin, sir. Perhaps that is not a nice thing to say. But I like men with big throats best. Big, thick, red throats . . .'

He took something from his coat, looked at it closely and ran it across his wet finger. Then he moved it slowly up and down over his open hand.

'This is a little French razor,' he said quietly. 'Perhaps you know them. They do not cut very far into the throat but they

He took a razor from his coat, looked at it closely and ran it across his wet finger.

cut very cleanly, I find. In just a minute, I am going to show you how well they cut. But first, I must ask the question that I always ask: is the razor to your liking, sir?'

He stood up: small and very dangerous. He walked over to Hewson as slowly and quietly as a cat going after a bird.

'Please be so good as to put your head back a little. Thank you. And now a little more. Just a little more. Ah, thank you! That's right, Monsieur . . . Thank you . . . Thank you . . .'

♦

At one end of the room is a small window. In the daytime it gives a weak light. After the sun comes up, this new light makes the room seem sadder and dirtier than before.

Raymond Hewson's face is up, ready for the razor. There is no cut on his throat or anywhere on his body. But he is dead.

The waxwork figures stand in their places, with unseeing eyes. Soon the visitors are going to arrive. They are going to walk round, looking at this figure or that. But today, in the centre of the room, Hewson sits with his head far back in his armchair. His face is up, ready for the razor. There is no cut on his throat or anywhere on his body. But he is cold. Dead.

And Dr Bourdette watches the dead man from his stand, without any show of feeling. He does not move. He cannot move. But then, he is only a waxwork.

ACTIVITIES

The Lady or the Tiger?, pages 1–3

Before you read

1 Look at the Word list at the back of the book. Answer these questions.

    a Which of these can't move – a waxwork or a king?

    b Which of these do men use in the morning – a razor or a handle?

    c You are suddenly afraid. Do you scream or sneeze?

    d Which is black and orange and dangerous – a lady or a tiger?

2 Read the Introduction to this book. Which story is about

    a a man and a murderer?   **b** an angry father?

    c a man in a bed?

3 The first story is about a king, a lady and a tiger. What will happen, do you think?

While you read

4 Choose the right words in *italics*.

    a The King has a big problem with *his people/wrongdoers*.

    b *The King's family/The people* work hard and build the stadium.

    c People will *play games/watch wrongdoers* in the stadium.

    d *A beautiful woman/The wrongdoer's wife* is behind one door.

    e *A dangerous man/A tiger* is behind another door.

    f The people are happy when the man opens the *right/wrong* door.

    g They go home sadly when the man chooses the *lady/tiger*.

    h The King's plan *works/doesn't work*.

After you read

5 Do you think the King's plan is a good plan? Why (not)?

6 Work with a friend. Have this conversation.

    Student A: You are a wrongdoer. Tomorrow you have to go into the stadium. How can you choose the right door?

    Student B: You are the friend of a wrongdoer. How can he/she choose the right door?

The Lady or the Tiger?, pages 4–9

Before you read

7 Discuss the questions.

    a The people don't like the king's plan. Will they do anything?

    b An important person comes into the story now. Who will it be?

While you read

8 Who is the sentence about? Put the right word in the sentence.

    a The King's .... is strong, clever and dangerous.

    b The King's .... can't marry the King's daughter.

    c The .... catches the lovers.

    d The King's .... put the young man in a dark room.

    e The King's .... daughter will be behind one door.

    f The King's .... moves her finger to the left.

After you read

9 Which of these things do you think will happen?

    a The tiger will eat the King's gardener.

    b The driver's daughter will marry the King's gardener.

    c The King's daughter will kill the driver's daughter.

10 Make sentences about three of the people in the story. Use these words:

    a red hair/green eyes/clever/dangerous/famous smile

    b tall/strong/blue-black hair/white teeth/not rich

    c young/beautiful/rich brown hair

11 Why does this story end without an end, do you think?

Miss Bracegirdle's Night of Fear, pages 10–16

Before you read

12 Answer these questions.

    a Does Miss Bracegirdle have a husband? How do you know?

    b She is staying in a hotel and she is going to have a 'night of fear'. What will happen, do you think?

While you read

13 Are these sentences right (✓) or wrong (✗)?

    a Miss Bracegirdle is staying in a hotel in South America.   .....

    b She asks the girl to bring her an early breakfast.   .....

    c She saw her sister Annie last year.   .....

    d She does not often have holidays in Europe.   .....

    e She pulls the door-handle off the door, so she can't
open it.   .....

    f She screams when she sees the man.   .....

    g She lies down under the bed.   .....

    h She sneezes, and the man jumps out of bed.   .....

After you read

14 Miss Bracegirdle nearly dies of fear three times that night. What three things happen?

15 You are in the room. The door handle is in your hand. The man is in the bed. Everybody in the hotel is sleeping. What do *you* do?

Miss Bracegirdle's Night of Fear, pages 17–23

Before you read

16 Do you think one of these things will happen?

    a The man will wake up and jump on Miss Bracegirdle.

    b The police will think Miss Bracegirdle is the murderer.

    What do *you* think will happen?

While you read

17 What happens first? What happens next? Write numbers 1–7.

    a She finds a knife in the man's jacket.   .....

    b She remembers her washing things are in the
man's room.   .....

    c She sends a letter.   .....

    d She wakes up and sees that it is eleven o'clock.   .....

    e Somebody puts shoes down outside the door.   .....

    f The girl tells her that the man was Boldhu,
a famous killer.   .....

    g The girl tells her about a dead man in Room 117.   .....

18 Why doesn't Miss Bracegirdle tell anybody about her night of fear? And why is her face red when she sends her letter?

19 Put these words in the newspaper story about the dead man.
dead English famous hear kill knife police saw see why

KILLER DEAD IN HOTEL BED!

Early this morning, a young woman called the (a)..... to the Hotel Carlton. They found a (b)..... man in one of the hotel rooms. They found a name and a (c)..... in the man's jacket. He was the (d)..... killer, Boldhu! 'I screamed when I (e)..... him!' said the woman. 'Boldhu – here!' The police have some questions: (f)..... did he have a knife? Was he going to (g)..... somebody? We spoke to an (h)..... woman in the hotel. 'I didn't (i)..... or (j)..... anything,' she said.

The Waxwork, pages 24–30

Before you read

20 Discuss these questions.

    a In this story, a newspaper man plans to stay a night with some waxworks. They are figures of famous murderers. He wants to write a story and sell it for money. Is this a good idea or not?

    b You can see waxworks of famous people at Madame Tussaud's in London. Would you like to visit Madame Tussaud's?

While you read

21 Write the answers to these questions.

    a How much money is Mr Marriner going
to pay? ....

    b Was there really a fire in the Murderer's
Room? ....

    c Are the murderers all men? ....

    d Which murderer is perhaps not dead? ....

    e In which city did Dr Bourdette cut throats? ....

    f Where are the police looking for Dr
Bourdette? ....

g Who could send people to sleep with his
  eyes?   ....

22 Work with a friend. Have this conversation.

  Student A: You work for a newspaper. You want to know about
          Dr Bourdette. Ask about these things: his name? his
          job? where he comes from? small or tall? fat or thin?
          glasses? strange clothes?

  Student B: You work for the police. Answer the questions.

The Waxwork, pages 30–39

Before you read

23 What do you think about these questions?

  a Will Hewson feel afraid in the night?
  b Will he be there in the morning?
  c Would you like to stay a night in the Murderers' Room?

While you read

24 Choose the right words in *italics* in each sentence.

  a Hewson feels *happier / more afraid* after the night watchman
     brings the chair.
  b He hears *a lot of sounds / nothing* in the big, dark room.
  c When Hewson's eyes meet Dr Bourdette's, *Hewson / the
     murderer* turns away.
  d He thinks Crippen *is / isn't* moving.
  e He stays because he *wants the money / can't leave*.
  f He *has to / wants to* look at Bourdette.
  g Bourdette *is a waxwork / put the waxwork away*.
  h Bourdette *likes / doesn't like* Hewson's throat very much.

After you read

25 Work with a friend. Have this conversation.

  Student A: You are Mr Marriner. What happened, do you think?
          Tell the night watchman.

  Student B: You are the night watchman. What did you see and
          hear? Tell Mr Marriner.

26 Discuss these questions.

    a Did you feel afraid when you read the stories?

    b Which story did you like best?

Writing

27 Write an end for 'The Lady or the Tiger?'

28 You are the King in the story. You are a strong King with strong ideas. How must your people live their lives? Write about five things. Use the word *must*.

29 Miss Bracegirdle doesn't tell her brother about her 'night of fear'. But she tells her sister, Annie. Annie asks her questions. Write their conversation.

30 You are Miss Bracegirdle. You meet your sister Annie. You stay in France for a week at a different hotel. Write another postcard to your brother. You can tell him about the weather, Annie, and interesting places.

31 Look at the picture at the end of 'The Waxwork'. You are a policeman/woman. You saw Hewson's dead body, you studied the room and questioned people. Write your police notes. Say what you think happened.

32 Think about a different end for 'The Waxwork': Hewson doesn't die. Write his story for the newspaper.

33 Write about one of the pictures in the book. What is happening? What happened before? What is going to happen next in the story?

34 Do you know any other good stories of fear and suspense? Write about the story, or write a new story.

WORD LIST

body (n) The killer cut the man's head from his *body*.

choose (v) *Choose* the best answer: a, b or c.

fear (n) Some people have a *fear* of high places.

figure (n) The *figures* in the picture are jumping and dancing.

handle (n) He turned the *handle* and opened the door.

king (n) *King* Henry was a famous *king* of England.

lady (n) 'Woman' and '*lady*' are the same, but '*lady*' is more polite.

lie, lay (v) He wanted to *lie* down, so he *lay* on the bed.

lucky, unlucky (adj) He was good at the game but he was *unlucky* and didn't win.

suspense (n) There's a lot of *suspense* in the story: the reader is always waiting for the next exciting thing.

murder (v/n) She *murdered* her husband, and the police never caught her.

must (v) We don't want to wake him, so we *must* be quiet.

wrongdoer (n) Every country has police because every country has *wrongdoers*.

razor (n) He cut his face accidentally with a *razor*.

scream (v/n) She was very afraid and she *screamed* loudly.

sneeze (v/n) He *sneezed* loudly: 'Ashoo! Ashoo!'

stadium (n) Fifty thousand people watched the game in the big *stadium*.

throat (n) I've got a cold and my *throat* hurts.

tiger (n) *Tigers* are dangerous 'big cats' from Asia.

waxwork (n) *Waxworks* and living people look nearly the same.

Treasure Island
Robert Louis Stevenson

A young boy, Jim Hawkins, lives quietly by the sea with his mother and father. One day, Billy Bones comes to lives with them and from that day everything is different. Jim meets Long Jim Silver, a man with one leg, and Jim and Long John Silver go far across the sea in a ship called the *Hispaniola* to Treasure Island.

The Mummy

"Imhotep is half-dead and will be half-dead for all time."

The Mummy is an exciting movie. Imhotep dies in Ancient Egypt. 3,700 years later Rick O'Connell finds him. Imhotep is very dangerous. Can O'Connell send him back to the dead?

The Last of the Mohicans
James Fenimore Cooper

Uncas is the last of the Mohican Indians. He is with his father and Hawkeye when they meet Heyward. Heyward is taking the two young daughters of a British colonel to their father. But a Huron Indian who hates the British is near. Will the girls see their father again?

There are hundreds of Penguin Readers to choose from – world classics, film adaptations, modern-day crime and adventure, short stories, biographies, American classics, non-fiction, plays ...

For a complete list of all Penguin Readers titles, please contact your local Pearson Longman office or visit our website.

www.penguinreaders.com

Pirates of the Caribbean
The Curse of the Black Pearl

Elizabeth lives on a Caribbean island, a very dangerous place.
A young blacksmith is interested in her, but pirates are interested
too. Where do the pirates come from and what do they want? Is
there really a curse on their ship? And why can't they enjoy their
gold?

Robin Hood

Robin Hood robbed rich people and gave the money to the poor.
He fought against the greedy Sheriff of Nottingham and bad Prince
John and defended the beautiful Lady Marian. *Robin Hood is a
folk-hero and the story is supposed to be true!*

Moby Dick
Herman Melville

Moby Dick is the most dangerous whale in the oceans. Captain
Ahab fought him and lost a leg. Now he hates Moby Dick. He
wants to kill him. But can Captain Ahab and his men find the
great white whale? A young sailor, Ishmael, tells the story of their
exciting and dangerous trip.

*There are hundreds of Penguin Readers to choose from – world classics,
film adaptations, modern-day crime and adventure, short stories,
biographies, American classics, non-fiction, plays ...*

For a complete list of all Penguin Readers titles, please contact your local
Pearson Longman office or visit our website.

www.penguinreaders.com

Longman Dictionaries

Express yourself with confidence!

Longman has led the way in ELT dictionaries since 1935. We constantly talk to students and teachers around the world to find out what they need from a learner's dictionary.

Why choose a Longman dictionary?

Easy to understand

Longman invented the Defining Vocabulary – 2000 of the most common words which are used to write the definitions in our dictionaries. So Longman definitions are always clear and easy to understand.

Real, natural English

All Longman dictionaries contain natural examples taken from real-life that help explain the meaning of a word and show you how to use it in context.

Avoid common mistakes

Longman dictionaries are written specially for learners, and we make sure that you get all the help you need to avoid common mistakes. We analyse typical learners' mistakes and include notes on how to avoid them.

Innovative CD-ROMs

Longman are leaders in dictionary CD-ROM innovation. Did you know that a dictionary CD-ROM includes features to help improve your pronunciation, help you practice for exams and improve your writing skills?

For details of all Longman dictionaries, and to choose the one that's right for you, visit our website:

www.longman.com/dictionaries